BECAUSE
OF
LOVE

LINDA ELLIS

authorHOUSE®

AuthorHouse™
1663 Liberty Drive
Bloomington, IN 47403
www.authorhouse.com
Phone: 1 (800) 839-8640

Published by AuthorHouse 11/21/2019

ISBN: 978-1-7283-3704-3 (sc)
ISBN: 978-1-7283-3702-9 (hc)
ISBN: 978-1-7283-3703-6 (e)

Print information available on the last page.

*Scripture quotations marked NLT are taken from the Holy Bible, New Living
Translation, copyright © 1996, 2004, 2007. Used by permission of Tyndale House
Publishers, Inc. Carol Stream, Illinois 60188. All rights reserved. Website*

This book is printed on acid-free paper.

INTRODUCTION

JOHN 3:16

**FOR GOD SO LOVED THE WORLD,
THAT HE GAVE HIS ONLY
BEGOTTEN SON, THAT WHOSOEVER
BELIEVETH IN HIM SHALL NOT
PERISH, BUT HAVE EVERLASING LIFE.**

PERSONAL INFORMATION

Journal Year_____

Name_____
Address_____
Telephone E-Mail_____

IN CASE OF EMERGENCY NOTIFY

Name_____
Address_____
Telephone_____ **Relationship**_____

JANUARY

For I Know the plan I have
for you, "says the Lord.
They are plans for good
and not disaster to give
you a future and a hope

Jeremiah 29:11

DAY 2
Notes _____

_____

_____

_____

_____

_____

_____

_____

_____

_____

_____

_____

_____

_____

_____

_____

_____

_____

_____

_____

_____

_____

_____

_____

DAY 3
Notes

DAY 4
Notes

DAY 5
Notes _____

DAY 6
Notes _____

_____

_____

_____

_____

_____

_____

_____

_____

_____

_____

_____

_____

_____

_____

_____

_____

_____

_____

_____

_____

_____

_____

_____

_____

DAY 7
Notes _____

_____

_____

_____

_____

_____

_____

_____

_____

_____

_____

_____

_____

_____

_____

_____

_____

_____

_____

_____

_____

_____

_____

_____

_____

_____

_____

DAY 8
Notes _____

_____

_____

_____

_____

_____

_____

_____

_____

_____

_____

_____

_____

_____

_____

_____

_____

_____

_____

_____

_____

_____

DAY 9
Notes

DAY 10
Notes

DAY 11
Notes

DAY 12
Notes

DAY 13
Notes _____

_____

_____

_____

_____

_____

_____

_____

_____

_____

_____

_____

_____

_____

_____

_____

_____

_____

_____

_____

_____

_____

_____

_____

_____

DAY 14
Notes

DAY 15
Notes

DAY 16
Notes

DAY 17
Notes _____

_____

_____

_____

_____

_____

_____

_____

_____

_____

_____

_____

_____

_____

_____

_____

_____

_____

_____

_____

_____

_____

_____

_____

_____

_____

DAY 18
Notes

DAY 19
Notes

DAY 20
Notes

DAY 21
Notes _____

_____
_____
_____
_____
_____
_____
_____
_____
_____
_____
_____
_____
_____
_____
_____
_____
_____
_____
_____
_____
_____
_____

DAY 22
Notes

_____

_____

_____

_____

_____

_____

_____

_____

_____

_____

_____

_____

_____

_____

_____

_____

_____

_____

_____

_____

_____

_____

Notes _____

_____

_____

_____

_____

_____

_____

_____

_____

_____

_____

_____

_____

_____

_____

_____

_____

_____

_____

_____

_____

_____

_____

_____

_____

DAY 24
Notes

DAY 25
Notes _____

_____

_____

_____

_____

_____

_____

_____

_____

_____

_____

_____

_____

_____

_____

_____

_____

_____

_____

_____

_____

_____

_____

DAY 26
Notes

DAY 27
Notes

28

DAY 28
Notes

DAY 29
Notes

DAY 30
Notes

DAY 31
Notes _____

_____

_____

_____

_____

_____

_____

_____

_____

_____

_____

_____

_____

_____

_____

_____

_____

_____

_____

_____

_____

_____

_____

FEBRUARY

There are three things
that will endure, faith,
hope and love and the
greatest of these is love.

1 Corinthians 13:13

DAY 1
Notes

_____
_____
_____
_____
_____
_____
_____
_____
_____
_____
_____
_____
_____
_____
_____
_____
_____
_____
_____
_____
_____
_____
_____

DAY 2
Notes

DAY 3
Notes

DAY 4
Notes

DAY 5
Notes

DAY 6
Notes

_____

DAY 7
Notes

DAY 8
Notes

DAY 9
Notes

DAY 10
Notes

DAY 11
Notes _____

_____

_____

_____

_____

_____

_____

_____

_____

_____

_____

_____

_____

_____

_____

_____

_____

_____

_____

_____

_____

_____

_____

_____

_____

_____

DAY 12
Notes _____

_____
_____
_____
_____
_____
_____
_____
_____
_____
_____
_____
_____
_____
_____
_____
_____
_____
_____
_____
_____
_____
_____
_____

DAY 13
Notes

DAY 14
Notes

DAY 15
Notes

DAY 16
Notes

DAY 17
Notes _____

_____

_____

_____

_____

_____

_____

_____

_____

_____

_____

_____

_____

_____

_____

_____

_____

_____

_____

_____

_____

_____

_____

DAY 18
Notes

DAY 19
Notes _____

_____

_____

_____

_____

_____

_____

_____

_____

_____

_____

_____

_____

_____

_____

_____

_____

_____

_____

_____

_____

_____

_____

_____

DAY 20
Notes

DAY 21
Notes _____

_____

_____

_____

_____

_____

_____

_____

_____

_____

_____

_____

_____

_____

_____

_____

_____

_____

_____

_____

_____

_____

_____

_____

_____

DAY 22
Notes _____

_____

_____

_____

_____

_____

_____

_____

_____

_____

_____

_____

_____

_____

_____

_____

_____

_____

_____

_____

_____

_____

_____

_____

DAY 23
Notes

DAY 24
Notes _____

DAY 25
Notes

DAY 26
Notes

DAY 27
Notes _____

_____

_____

_____

_____

_____

_____

_____

_____

_____

_____

_____

_____

_____

_____

_____

_____

_____

_____

_____

_____

_____

_____

_____

DAY 28
Notes

DAY 29
Notes _____

_____

_____

_____

_____

_____

_____

_____

_____

_____

_____

_____

_____

_____

_____

_____

_____

_____

_____

_____

_____

_____

_____

_____

MARCH

God demonstrates his
own love for us in this,
while we were still sinners,
Christ died for us.

Romans 5:8

DAY 1
Notes _____

_____

_____

_____

_____

_____

_____

_____

_____

_____

_____

_____

_____

_____

_____

_____

_____

_____

_____

_____

_____

DAY 2
Notes

DAY 3
Notes _____

DAY 4
Notes

DAY 5
Notes _____

_____

_____

_____

_____

_____

_____

_____

_____

_____

_____

_____

_____

_____

_____

_____

_____

_____

_____

_____

_____

_____

_____

_____

_____

DAY 6
Notes

DAY 7
Notes

DAY 8
Notes

DAY 9
Notes

DAY 10
Notes

DAY 11
Notes _____

_____

_____

_____

_____

_____

_____

_____

_____

_____

_____

_____

_____

_____

_____

_____

_____

_____

_____

_____

_____

_____

DAY 12
Notes

DAY 13
Notes _____

_____
_____
_____
_____
_____
_____
_____
_____
_____
_____
_____
_____
_____
_____
_____
_____
_____
_____
_____
_____
_____
_____
_____

DAY 14
Notes _____

DAY 15
Notes _____

_____

_____

_____

_____

_____

_____

_____

_____

_____

_____

_____

_____

_____

_____

_____

_____

_____

_____

_____

_____

_____

_____

DAY 16
Notes

DAY 17
Notes _____

_____

_____

_____

_____

_____

_____

_____

_____

_____

_____

_____

_____

_____

_____

_____

_____

_____

_____

_____

_____

_____

_____

_____

_____

DAY 18
Notes

DAY 19
Notes

DAY 20
Notes

DAY 21
Notes _____

_____

_____

_____

_____

_____

_____

_____

_____

_____

_____

_____

_____

_____

_____

_____

_____

_____

_____

_____

_____

_____

_____

DAY 22
Notes

DAY 23
Notes _____

_____
_____
_____
_____
_____
_____
_____
_____
_____
_____
_____
_____
_____
_____
_____
_____
_____
_____
_____
_____
_____
_____
_____

DAY 24
Notes _____

DAY 25
Notes _____

_____

_____

_____

_____

_____

_____

_____

_____

_____

_____

_____

_____

_____

_____

_____

_____

_____

_____

_____

_____

_____

_____

_____

DAY 26
Notes

DAY 27
Notes _____

_____

_____

_____

_____

_____

_____

_____

_____

_____

_____

_____

_____

_____

_____

_____

_____

_____

_____

_____

_____

_____

_____

DAY 28
Notes

DAY 29
Notes

DAY 30
Notes

DAY 31
Notes

APRIL

I am the resurrection and
the life. He who believes in
me will live, even though he
dies, and whoever lives and
believes in me will never die.

John 11:25-26

DAY 1
Notes _____

_____

_____

_____

_____

_____

_____

_____

_____

_____

_____

_____

_____

_____

_____

_____

_____

_____

_____

_____

_____

_____

_____

_____

_____

DAY 2
Notes

DAY 3
Notes

DAY 4
Notes

DAY 5
Notes _____

_____

_____

_____

_____

_____

_____

_____

_____

_____

_____

_____

_____

_____

_____

_____

_____

_____

_____

_____

_____

_____

_____

_____

_____

_____

DAY 6
Notes

DAY 7
Notes _____

_____

_____

_____

_____

_____

_____

_____

_____

_____

_____

_____

_____

_____

_____

_____

_____

_____

_____

_____

_____

_____

_____

_____

_____

_____

DAY 8
Notes _____

DAY 9
Notes _____

_____

_____

_____

_____

_____

_____

_____

_____

_____

_____

_____

_____

_____

_____

_____

_____

_____

_____

_____

_____

_____

_____

DAY 10
Notes

DAY 11
Notes _____

_____

_____

_____

_____

_____

_____

_____

_____

_____

_____

_____

_____

_____

_____

_____

_____

_____

_____

_____

_____

_____

DAY 12
Notes

DAY 13
Notes _____

_____
_____
_____
_____
_____
_____
_____
_____
_____
_____
_____
_____
_____
_____
_____
_____
_____
_____
_____
_____
_____
_____
_____
_____
_____

DAY 14
Notes

DAY 15
Notes _____

_____
_____
_____
_____
_____
_____
_____
_____
_____
_____
_____
_____
_____
_____
_____
_____
_____
_____
_____
_____
_____
_____
_____

DAY 16
Notes

DAY 17
Notes

DAY 18
Notes _____

DAY 19
Notes

DAY 20
Notes _____

_____

_____

_____

_____

_____

_____

_____

_____

_____

_____

_____

_____

_____

_____

_____

_____

_____

_____

_____

_____

_____

_____

_____

_____

DAY 21
Notes _____

_____

_____

_____

_____

_____

_____

_____

_____

_____

_____

_____

_____

_____

_____

_____

_____

_____

_____

_____

_____

_____

_____

DAY 22
Notes _____

DAY 23
Notes _____

DAY 24
Notes

DAY 25
Notes

DAY 26
Notes _____

DAY 27
Notes _____

_____

_____

_____

_____

_____

_____

_____

_____

_____

_____

_____

_____

_____

_____

_____

_____

_____

_____

_____

_____

_____

_____

DAY 28
Notes

DAY 29
Notes

DAY 30
Notes

MAY

I will comfort you there
as a child is comforted
by its Mother.

Isaiah 66:13

DAY 1
Notes

DAY 2
Notes _____

DAY 3
Notes

DAY 4
Notes _____

_____

_____

_____

_____

_____

_____

_____

_____

_____

_____

_____

_____

_____

_____

_____

_____

_____

_____

_____

_____

_____

_____

_____

DAY 5
Notes

DAY 6
Notes

DAY 7
Notes

DAY 8
Notes

DAY 9
Notes

DAY 10
Notes

DAY 11
Notes

DAY 12
Notes

DAY 13
Notes

DAY 14
Notes

DAY 15
Notes

DAY 16
Notes

DAY 17
Notes

Notes _____

_____

_____

_____

_____

_____

_____

_____

_____

_____

_____

_____

_____

_____

_____

_____

_____

_____

_____

_____

_____

_____

_____

_____

_____

_____

DAY 19
Notes

DAY 20
Notes

_____

_____

_____

_____

_____

_____

_____

_____

_____

_____

_____

_____

_____

_____

_____

_____

_____

_____

_____

_____

_____

_____

DAY 21
Notes

DAY 22
Notes _____

_____

_____

_____

_____

_____

_____

_____

_____

_____

_____

_____

_____

_____

_____

_____

_____

_____

_____

_____

_____

_____

_____

DAY 23
Notes

DAY 24
Notes

_____

_____

_____

_____

_____

_____

_____

_____

_____

_____

_____

_____

_____

_____

_____

_____

_____

_____

_____

_____

_____

_____

DAY 25
Notes

DAY 26
Notes

DAY 27
Notes

DAY 28
Notes

DAY 29
Notes

DAY 30
Notes _____

_____

_____

_____

_____

_____

_____

_____

_____

_____

_____

_____

_____

_____

_____

_____

_____

_____

_____

_____

_____

_____

_____

DAY 31
Notes

JUNE

My faithful love will be
with him..He will call out to
me. "You are my father, my
God, the Rock my Savior."

Psalm 89: 24-26

DAY 1
Notes _____

DAY 2
Notes

DAY 3
Notes

DAY 4
Notes _____

_____

_____

_____

_____

_____

_____

_____

_____

_____

_____

_____

_____

_____

_____

_____

_____

_____

_____

_____

_____

_____

_____

_____

DAY 5
Notes

DAY 6
Notes _____

_____

_____

_____

_____

_____

_____

_____

_____

_____

_____

_____

_____

_____

_____

_____

_____

_____

_____

_____

_____

_____

_____

_____

_____

_____

DAY 7
Notes

DAY 8
Notes _____

_____

_____

_____

_____

_____

_____

_____

_____

_____

_____

_____

_____

_____

_____

_____

_____

_____

_____

_____

_____

_____

_____

DAY 9
Notes

DAY 10
Notes _____

_____

_____

_____

_____

_____

_____

_____

_____

_____

_____

_____

_____

_____

_____

_____

_____

_____

_____

_____

_____

_____

_____

_____

DAY 11
Notes

DAY 12
Notes

DAY 13
Notes

DAY 14
Notes

DAY 15
Notes

DAY 16
Notes

DAY 17
Notes

DAY 18
Notes

DAY 19
Notes

DAY 20
Notes _____

_____

_____

_____

_____

_____

_____

_____

_____

_____

_____

_____

_____

_____

_____

_____

_____

_____

_____

_____

_____

_____

_____

_____

DAY 21
Notes

DAY 22
Notes

DAY 23
Notes

DAY 24
Notes

_____

_____

_____

_____

_____

_____

_____

_____

_____

_____

_____

_____

_____

_____

_____

_____

_____

_____

_____

_____

_____

_____

_____

_____

_____

DAY 25
Notes

DAY 26
Notes

DAY 27
Notes

DAY 28
Notes _____

_____

_____

_____

_____

_____

_____

_____

_____

_____

_____

_____

_____

_____

_____

_____

_____

_____

_____

_____

_____

_____

_____

_____

_____

_____

DAY 29
Notes

DAY 30
Notes

JULY

**We love because he
first loved us.**

1 John 4:19

DAY 1
Notes _____

_____

_____

_____

_____

_____

_____

_____

_____

_____

_____

_____

_____

_____

_____

_____

_____

_____

_____

_____

_____

_____

_____

DAY 2
Notes

DAY 3
Notes

DAY 4
Notes

DAY 5
Notes

DAY 6
Notes

DAY 8
Notes

DAY 9
Notes _____

_____
_____
_____
_____
_____
_____
_____
_____
_____
_____
_____
_____
_____
_____
_____
_____
_____
_____
_____
_____
_____
_____
_____
_____
_____

DAY 10
Notes

DAY 11
Notes _____

DAY 12
Notes

DAY 13
Notes

DAY 14
Notes _____

DAY 15
Notes _____

_____
_____
_____
_____
_____
_____
_____
_____
_____
_____
_____
_____
_____
_____
_____
_____
_____
_____
_____
_____
_____
_____
_____

DAY 16
Notes

DAY 17
Notes _____

_____

_____

_____

_____

_____

_____

_____

_____

_____

_____

_____

_____

_____

_____

_____

_____

_____

_____

_____

_____

_____

_____

_____

DAY 18
Notes

DAY 19
Notes _____

_____

_____

_____

_____

_____

_____

_____

_____

_____

_____

_____

_____

_____

_____

_____

_____

_____

_____

_____

_____

_____

_____

_____

DAY 20
Notes

DAY 21
Notes _____

_____

_____

_____

_____

_____

_____

_____

_____

_____

_____

_____

_____

_____

_____

_____

_____

_____

_____

_____

_____

_____

_____

_____

DAY 22
Notes

DAY 23
Notes _____

_____

_____

_____

_____

_____

_____

_____

_____

_____

_____

_____

_____

_____

_____

_____

_____

_____

_____

_____

_____

_____

_____

_____

DAY 24
Notes

DAY 25
Notes

DAY 26
Notes

DAY 27
Notes

DAY 28
Notes

DAY 29
Notes

DAY 30
Notes

DAY 31
Notes

AUGUST

I will heal their waywardness
and love them freely.

Hosea 14:4

DAY 1
Notes

_____

_____

_____

_____

_____

_____

_____

_____

_____

_____

_____

_____

_____

_____

_____

_____

_____

_____

_____

_____

_____

_____

DAY 2
Notes

DAY 3
Notes _____

_____

_____

_____

_____

_____

_____

_____

_____

_____

_____

_____

_____

_____

_____

_____

_____

_____

_____

_____

_____

_____

_____

_____

_____

DAY 4
Notes

DAY 5
Notes _____

_____

_____

_____

_____

_____

_____

_____

_____

_____

_____

_____

_____

_____

_____

_____

_____

_____

_____

_____

_____

_____

_____

_____

DAY 6
Notes

DAY 7
Notes

DAY 8
Notes

DAY 9
Notes

DAY 10
Notes

DAY 11
Notes

DAY 12
Notes _____

DAY 13
Notes _____

_____
_____
_____
_____
_____
_____
_____
_____
_____
_____
_____
_____
_____
_____
_____
_____
_____
_____
_____
_____
_____
_____
_____
_____

DAY 14
Notes _____

_____

_____

_____

_____

_____

_____

_____

_____

_____

_____

_____

_____

_____

_____

_____

_____

_____

_____

_____

_____

_____

_____

_____

_____

DAY 15
Notes

DAY 16
Notes _____

DAY 17
Notes

DAY 18
Notes _____

_____

_____

_____

_____

_____

_____

_____

_____

_____

_____

_____

_____

_____

_____

_____

_____

_____

_____

_____

_____

_____

_____

_____

DAY 19
Notes

DAY 21
Notes _____

_____

_____

_____

_____

_____

_____

_____

_____

_____

_____

_____

_____

_____

_____

_____

_____

_____

_____

_____

_____

_____

DAY 22
Notes

DAY 23
Notes

DAY 24
Notes

DAY 25
Notes

DAY 26
Notes

DAY 27
Notes _____

_____

_____

_____

_____

_____

_____

_____

_____

_____

_____

_____

_____

_____

_____

_____

_____

_____

_____

_____

_____

_____

_____

_____

_____

DAY 28
Notes _____

DAY 29
Notes

DAY 30
Notes _____

DAY 31
Notes

SEPTEMBER

I pray that you, being rooted and established in love, may grasp how wide and long and high and deep is the love of Christ.

Ephesians 3:17-18

DAY 2
Notes

DAY 3
Notes

DAY 4
Notes

DAY 5
Notes

DAY 6
Notes

DAY 7
Notes

_____

_____

_____

_____

_____

_____

_____

_____

_____

_____

_____

_____

_____

_____

_____

_____

_____

_____

_____

_____

_____

_____

_____

DAY 8
Notes

DAY 9
Notes
_____

DAY 10
Notes _____

DAY 11
Notes _____

DAY 12
Notes

DAY 13
Notes _____

_____

_____

_____

_____

_____

_____

_____

_____

_____

_____

_____

_____

_____

_____

_____

_____

_____

_____

_____

_____

_____

_____

_____

DAY 14
Notes

DAY 15
Notes

DAY 16
Notes

DAY 17
Notes _____

_____
_____
_____
_____
_____
_____
_____
_____
_____
_____
_____
_____
_____
_____
_____
_____
_____
_____
_____
_____
_____
_____
_____

DAY 18
Notes

DAY 19
Notes

DAY 20
Notes

DAY 21
Notes

DAY 22
Notes

DAY 23
Notes

DAY 24
Notes

DAY 25
Notes _____

_____

_____

_____

_____

_____

_____

_____

_____

_____

_____

_____

_____

_____

_____

_____

_____

_____

_____

_____

_____

_____

_____

_____

DAY 26
Notes

DAY 27
Notes

DAY 28
Notes

DAY 29
Notes

DAY 30
Notes

_____

OCTOBER

God has said, "Never
will I leave you; never
will I forsake you."

Hebrews13:5

DAY 1
Notes

DAY 2
Notes

DAY 3
Notes

DAY 4
Notes

DAY 5
Notes

DAY 6
Notes _____

_____

_____

_____

_____

_____

_____

_____

_____

_____

_____

_____

_____

_____

_____

_____

_____

_____

_____

_____

_____

_____

_____

_____

_____

_____

DAY 7
Notes

DAY 8
Notes

DAY 9
Notes

293

DAY 10
Notes

DAY 11
Notes

DAY 12
Notes

DAY 13
Notes

297

DAY 15
Notes

DAY 16
Notes _____

_____
_____
_____
_____
_____
_____
_____
_____
_____
_____
_____
_____
_____
_____
_____
_____
_____
_____
_____
_____
_____
_____
_____
_____

DAY 17
Notes

DAY 18
Notes

DAY 19
Notes

DAY 20
Notes _____

_____

_____

_____

_____

_____

_____

_____

_____

_____

_____

_____

_____

_____

_____

_____

_____

_____

_____

_____

_____

_____

_____

_____

_____

_____

DAY 21
Notes

DAY 22
Notes

DAY 23
Notes

DAY 24
Notes

DAY 25
Notes

DAY 26
Notes

DAY 27
Notes

DAY 28
Notes

DAY 29
Notes

DAY 30
Notes _____

_____

_____

_____

_____

_____

_____

_____

_____

_____

_____

_____

_____

_____

_____

_____

_____

_____

_____

_____

_____

_____

_____

_____

_____

DAY 31
Notes _____

_____

_____

_____

_____

_____

_____

_____

_____

_____

_____

_____

_____

_____

_____

_____

_____

_____

_____

_____

_____

_____

_____

_____

NOVEMBER

Give thanks to the Lord,
for he is good! His faithful
love endures forever

Psalm 106:1

DAY 1
Notes

317

DAY 2
Notes

DAY 3
Notes

DAY 4
Notes

_____

_____

_____

_____

_____

_____

_____

_____

_____

_____

_____

_____

_____

_____

_____

_____

_____

_____

_____

_____

_____

_____

_____

DAY 5
Notes

DAY 6
Notes

DAY 7
Notes _____

_____

_____

_____

_____

_____

_____

_____

_____

_____

_____

_____

_____

_____

_____

_____

_____

_____

_____

_____

_____

_____

_____

_____

DAY 8
Notes
_____

DAY 9
Notes

DAY 11
Notes

DAY 12
Notes _____

_____

_____

_____

_____

_____

_____

_____

_____

_____

_____

_____

_____

_____

_____

_____

_____

_____

_____

_____

_____

_____

_____

_____

_____

_____

DAY 13
Notes

DAY 14
Notes

DAY 15
Notes

DAY 16
Notes

DAY 18
Notes

DAY 19
Notes

DAY 20
Notes

DAY 21
Notes _____

_____

_____

_____

_____

_____

_____

_____

_____

_____

_____

_____

_____

_____

_____

_____

_____

_____

_____

_____

_____

_____

_____

_____

_____

_____

DAY 22
Notes

DAY 23
Notes

DAY 24
Notes

DAY 25
Notes

DAY 26
Notes

DAY 27
Notes

DAY 28
Notes

DAY 29
Notes

DAY 30
Notes

DECEMBER

Do not conform any longer
to the pattern of this world,
but be transformed by the
renewing of your mind.

Romans 12:2

DAY 1
Notes _____

_____

_____

_____

_____

_____

_____

_____

_____

_____

_____

_____

_____

_____

_____

_____

_____

_____

_____

_____

_____

_____

_____

DAY 2
Notes

DAY 3
Notes _____

_____

_____

_____

_____

_____

_____

_____

_____

_____

_____

_____

_____

_____

_____

_____

_____

_____

_____

_____

_____

_____

_____

DAY 4
Notes

DAY 5
Notes

DAY 6
Notes

DAY 7
Notes _____

DAY 8
Notes _____

DAY 9
Notes

DAY 10
Notes

DAY 11
Notes _____

_____

_____

_____

_____

_____

_____

_____

_____

_____

_____

_____

_____

_____

_____

_____

_____

_____

_____

_____

_____

_____

DAY 12
Notes _____

_____

_____

_____

_____

_____

_____

_____

_____

_____

_____

_____

_____

_____

_____

_____

_____

_____

_____

_____

_____

_____

DAY 13
Notes

DAY 14
Notes

DAY 15
Notes _____

_____

_____

_____

_____

_____

_____

_____

_____

_____

_____

_____

_____

_____

_____

_____

_____

_____

_____

_____

_____

_____

_____

_____

_____

_____

DAY 16
Notes

DAY 17
Notes _____

_____

_____

_____

_____

_____

_____

_____

_____

_____

_____

_____

_____

_____

_____

_____

_____

_____

_____

_____

_____

_____

_____

_____

DAY 18
Notes

DAY 19
Notes _____

_____

_____

_____

_____

_____

_____

_____

_____

_____

_____

_____

_____

_____

_____

_____

_____

_____

_____

_____

_____

_____

_____

DAY 20
Notes _____

DAY 21
Notes _____

_____

_____

_____

_____

_____

_____

_____

_____

_____

_____

_____

_____

_____

_____

_____

_____

_____

_____

_____

_____

_____

_____

_____

_____

DAY 22
Notes

DAY 23
Notes

DAY 24
Notes

DAY 25
Notes

DAY 26
Notes

DAY 27
Notes _____

_____

_____

_____

_____

_____

_____

_____

_____

_____

_____

_____

_____

_____

_____

_____

_____

_____

_____

_____

_____

_____

_____

_____

DAY 28
Notes _____

_____

_____

_____

_____

_____

_____

_____

_____

_____

_____

_____

_____

_____

_____

_____

_____

_____

_____

_____

_____

_____

_____

_____

_____

_____

DAY 29
Notes

DAY 30
Notes

DAY 31
Notes

Printed in the United States
By Bookmasters